de·moc·ra·cy [diH-MOK-ruH-See]

NOUN, PLURAL de·moc·ra·cies.

1. government by the people; a form of government in which the supreme power is vested in the people and exercised directly by them or by their elected agents under a free electoral system.

2 having such a form of government: The United States and Canada are democracies.

3. a state of society characterized by formal equality of rights and privileges.

4. political or social equality; democratic spirit.

5. the common people of a community as distinguished from any privileged class; the common people with respect to their political power.

Every four years, America is faced with a big decision.

# AMERICAN REVOLUTION for kids

*Presents:*

# THE PRESIDENTIAL ELECTION

**WRITTEN & ILLUSTRATED BY CHRISTOPHER TRIMARCO**

American citizens from all 50 states gather to vote for the next President of the United States of America.

As an American citizen, it is your constitutional right to vote.

What America doesn't tell you is that your vote in the presidential election doesn't actually matter.

The President of the United States of America is not determined by the popular vote of the citizens.

The results of the presidential election are actually determined by a group of elected officials called the Electoral College.

The Electoral College is made up of representatives from each state that ultimately votes to choose the president.

The number of electoral votes each state has is determined by how many members of congress it has.

So a presidential candidate could win the majority vote from the citizens but still lose the election.

Your vote in the presidential election is basically a glorified suggestion.

The major problem in the electoral process isn't so much the Electoral College, but the two party system that America has inadvertently adopted.

When you vote, you may choose to vote for any eligible candidate regardless of their political affiliation.

The Democrats and Republicans are the two major political parties in America.

Billions of dollars from both parties are spent on presidential campaigns. A lot of these funds come from donations made by the parties' supporters.

Some of these funds come from federal funding, which ultimately comes from the American tax-payers. No matter what political views they may have.

The Republican and Democratic parties each have their own values. Both parties claim to have the American people's best interests at heart.

Yet both parties are both very content spending billions upon billions of the people's money in order to further their own agenda.

Billions of dollars are wasted on things like "Affordable Health Care," gun control, and other things that a large percentage of the people do not agree with.

Billions are wasted that could help the homeless.

Billions to help the people that are losing their homes. Instead, government funds went to bailout the banks that were foreclosing people's homes.

Billions of dollars that could go towards the National Debt.

Billions of dollars are spent for these candidates to tell you over and over what they plan on doing…

...and when it comes time to actually do these things, they waste even more money trying to pass a bill to approve them.

When the candidate finally gets into office, the things that seemed so important during the campaign suddenly don't seem that important anymore…

…like bringing those that are still fighting for our "freedom" home.

*There are more of us, than there are of them…*

2014 **TRiMaRCO**

www.ingramcontent.com/pod-product-compliance
Lightning Source LLC
Chambersburg PA
CBHW061051290526
45796CB00003B/16